Truth be told, "Bonita's Kitchen" started many years ago! As a busy, working mom, feeding my husband & two hungry boys, I had to get creative in the kitchen. The *"Bonita's Kitchen"* you have come to know started when my son asked me to share my recipe for Homemade Bread with him on YouTube, so it was easy to watch any time. Turns out, more than just my son watched that video! From my kitchen to yours, it is my pleasure to give you a little taste of Traditional Newfoundland Cooking.

- - -

Bonita Hussey is originally from a small community called Upper Island Cove in Newfoundland, Canada. For 27 years, Bonita and her husband, Raymond lived in Yellowknife, Northwest Territories, raising their two boys, Bradley & Steven.

Bonita and her husband are now retired, and have moved "back home" to Newfoundland, where they spend their time FaceTiming with their grandchildren, filming episodes for *Bonita's Kitchen*, and enjoying the beautiful sights & sounds of Newfoundland. They often wonder, "where did we ever get the time to work?"

Bonita would like to thank her husband, two sons, daughters-in-law, grandchildren, mother, family and friends — for standing by her throughout the journey.

I would like to dedicate my first cook book to my Dad, Lemoine Coombs, who passed away in 2010. Miss You!

1

JIGGS DINNER

A Newfoundland Classic. Served with Pease Pudding.

Prep time 30 mins / **Cook time** 2 hours / **Serves** 4

INGREDIENTS

2 pieces salt beef or salt pork riblets

6 potatoes

1 head of cabbage quartered

1 medium turnip cut in slices

6 carrots

1 parsnip

1 medium onion

½ bag yellow split peas

1 tbsp Butter

Pinch Pepper to taste

VIEW ONLINE

bonitaskitchen.com/jiggs

1) Soak salt beef or salt pork riblets overnight in cold water, then boil in large boiler for 30 minutes; drain; add more cold water to lower the amount of salt on the beef then add 1 medium onion to pot.

2) Pour ½ bag of yellow split peas in a pudding bag and tie the top with a string, soak overnight then start cooking peas in your pudding bag with salt beef or salt pork riblets for about 1 hour, then check to see if split peas are cooked. *(Please note: You can remove the pudding bag from the pot or leave it in the water and add your vegetables with it.)*

3) Add cabbage and turnip to your pot, then boil for another 15 minutes.

4) Add potatoes, carrot and parsnip to your pot then boil for another 15 minutes or until potatoes are fork tender.

FOR THE PEASE PUDDING

1) Soak ½ bag of yellow split peas in cold water overnight in your pudding bag, remove pudding bag with peas from water then cook with the second boil of your salt beef.

2) When the salt beef or salt pork riblets and vegetables are cooked, remove pea bag from pot then cut the string from bag and pour all peas into a bowl, mash with butter and pepper to taste.

3) Remove all vegetables from pot; place in separate bowls.

3

BLUEBERRY DUFF

Boiled or steamed, served with Jiggs Dinner or as a dessert with the topping of your choice.

Prep time 10 mins / **Cook time** 1.5 hours / **Serves** 8

Boiler half-filled with water / Medium heat

INGREDIENTS

¼ cup butter

½ cup sugar

pinch of salt

1 egg (beaten)

¼ cup milk or ½ water

1 cup all-purpose flour

1½ tsp baking powder

1 cup fresh or frozen blueberries

½ tsp vanilla

VIEW ONLINE

bonitaskitchen.com/duff

1) Cream butter and sugar until light and fluffy. Stir in egg, milk, vanilla and sift in dry ingredients. mix well.

2) Fold in blueberries and place mixture into a prepared cotton pudding bag and tie tightly (allow ½" space at top of bag for expansion).

3) Boil for approx. 1 hour 15 minutes (medium to high boil). Check boiler to ensure you still have water in pot, *NEVER LET BOIL DRY.* You can also use a heat proof plastic tub, uncovered, with a foil bowl at the bottom of your boiler, this is to prevent plastic tub from touching the bottom of your boiler. Your water level should only reach the halfway mark of your plastic tub.

4) After your blueberry duff is cooked, remove from boiler and place upside down on a plate; remove from tub or cotton bag, cut in 8 - 10 pieces, serve with your desired toppings.

Bonita's Tip:
You can use butter or margarine, prepared cotton bag is when you dip the cotton bag into boiling water and place on a plate to scoop up your mixture to put in bag. You can also put it in a heat proof plastic tub with no cover and place in hot water with a spoon or foil bowl on the bottom to keep your plastic container from burning. Altrernatively, you may use a pudding tin rather than a tub.

TURKEY STUFFING WITH SAUSAGE

Serves 8 to 10

INGREDIENTS

1 Full Turkey (9 to10 lbs)

1 Pk Pure pork sausage

Dressing (stuffing)

2 to 3 cups bread crumbs

1 Medium onion

3 Tbsp butter or olive oil

1 Tbsp pure savoury

Pinch salt

Pinch pepper

Gravy

Turkey drippings

1 cup of stock or vegetable water from Jiggs dinner

1 Tbsp of gravy browning (optional)

¼ cup flour or corn starch

¼ cup cold water

1) Mix together bread crumbs, ½ of the chopped onion and butter or olive oil. Add savoury, salt and pepper. Mix together with your hand.

2) Put dressing (stuffing) into rear turkey cavity. In the neck cavity, squeeze the pork sausage and cover with the flaps of turkey skin.

3) Place turkey in roaster; top with broth from your boiled Jiggs dinner or vegetable stock. Add a pinch of salt & pepper and ½ of chopped onion. Cover turkey with a lid or foil wrap.

4) Place your turkey in your preheated oven and bake for 2 hours and 15 minutes or until golden brown, check every 30 minutes to base with its drippings.

5) When cooked, take turkey out of oven remove from roaster, place on a plate and cover until you are ready to carve the turkey.

6) After remove the dressing and sausage from each cavity of your turkey, cut the sausage in small pieces to serve with your meal.

7) Put roaster on stove top to make gravy.

Bonita's Tip:
Mix turkey drippings, stock/vegetable water and gravy browning together in roaster and let it come to a boil. Mix together in a Mason Jar (or similar) with a cover, your flour or corn starch then add cold water; shake well until there are no flour lumps. Once your roaster stock has come to a boil, mix in your flour/cornstarch mixture until broth thickens.

TURKEY CASSEROLE

Preheat oven 350º / **Prep time** 15 mins / **Cook time** 45 mins / **Serves** 8

INGREDIENTS

1½ Cups elbow noodles

1½ Cups Cooked Turkey
(chopped in small pieces)

1 Medium Chopped Onion

¾ Cup Frozen green peas

1 Cup Shredded cheese

1 Cup grated bread crumbs

1 Cup milk

½ Cup Hot water from
noodle boil

2 Tbsp Butter

2 Tbsp Flour

½ Tsp Sea salt in boiling pot
water

Olive oil

Salt and Pepper to taste

1) Start boiling the water for your noodles set the heat to medium, then add ½ tsp sea salt and 1 tsp olive oil to pot. When water is boiling add your noodles stirring occasionally.

2) On a medium heat, place a large saucepan and start to make your sauce. Add 2 tbsp butter, 1 tbsp olive oil, let melt, add chopped onions. Fry until onion is partially cooked.

3) Add 2 tbsp flour, mix until incorporated, add 1 cup of milk, ½ cup of hot water from your noodle boil, stir until thick. Add shredded cheese, salt and pepper to taste, continue stirring until mixed.

4) Back to the noodles, strain off all water and put in a large heat-proof bowl. Add the rest of your ingredients, frozen green peas, cooked turkey, sauce, sea salt and pepper to taste, mix together.

5) Oil your casserole dish with olive oil, then add your mixture spread evenly in pan, top with grated bread crumbs, you can season again if needed.

Bonita's Tip:
When making this dish you can use any amount of ingredients you desire. If you like to use different spices for your taste that works good as well. Make this recipe your own.

BAKED HAM

Preheat oven 350º / **Prep time** 15 mins / **Boiling time** 2 hours covered

Bake time 1 hour covered / **Serves** 6 to 8

INGREDIENTS

Boiler:

1 smoked picnic ham

1 medium onion (cubed)

1 Tbsp black peppercorns

Sauce:

1 can crushed pineapple or cubed

1 cup brown sugar

¼ cup cold water

1 Tbsp corn starch

Roaster:

1 medium onion sliced

1) In large boiler, add water until half full, add picnic ham, black pepper corns, onion, boil on medium heat for 2 hours.

2) After ham has boiled, remove carefully from boiler into a large bowl. Remove the net from ham; toss away fat.

3) Cut slices in the top of your ham, add 1 medium sliced onion to the bottom of your roaster.

4) Put your ham on top of onion in large roaster. Add 1 cup warm water.

5) In a small pot, add crushed pineapple, brown sugar, ¼ cup water, 1 Tbsp corn starch, cook on stovetop, medium heat, 5 minutes.

6) Pour sauce / glaze over top of ham; pinch of black pepper

7) Bake ham for 1 hour, then check ham; if you'd like to brown the top more, remove cover and let bake for another 15 minutes.

8) Remove from heat let rest for 10 minutes then remove from roaster. Place on plate to carve in slices. Pour remaining sauce in the roaster on the ham.

9) Top with 8 red cherries (optional; this is for presentation).

SCALLOP POTATOES

Preheat oven 350° / **Prep time** 10 mins / **Bake time** 40 mins / **Serves** 6

This creamy Scallop Potato recipe is so delicious, you'll be going back for thirds!

1) Peel and cut potatoes in thin slices; keep in cold water until ready to use.

2) Place small saucepan on stove top turn heat to medium.

3) Add 2 tbsp butter, let melt. Add 2 tbsp flour, stir until combined.

4) Add 1 cup milk, 2 cups shredded cheddar cheese, continue stirring until combined.

5) Mix together in a small bowl, ¼ cup cold water and 1 egg, stir into your saucepan, continue mixing until egg and water has combined with sauce.

6) Grate some black pepper in your sauce, continue boiling until thick, remove from heat.

7) In a glass baking dish, pour 1 tsp olive oil in dish, begin layering your potatoes, pour some sauce over them. Top with shredded cheddar cheese, grate more black pepper and sea salt.

8) Continue layering remainder of potatoes and sauce, top with more shredded cheddar cheese, place inoven at 350° for 40 minutes.

When scallop potatoes are baked, remove from oven, cover with foil wrap until ready to serve.

INGREDIENTS

4 Medium potatoes thinly sliced

3 Cups Shredded Cheddar Cheese

2 Tbsp butter

1 Large egg

1 Cup Milk

¼ Cup Water

2 Tbsp Flour

1 Tsp olive oil

Pinch Sea salt and pepper

TOUTONS, BANKERS & FROZIES

Prep time 20 minutes

Toutons, Bankers & Frozies are a wonderful treat made with the leftover dough from homemade bread.

View online: **bonitaskitchen.com/toutons**

Toutons / Bankers

1) Pre-heat your frying pan to medium heat and add 1 tbsp butter and 1 tbsp olive oil.

2) Cut small or large pieces of dough about half the size as your hand and pull apart to make a flat dough.

3) Place about 6 small pieces or 3 large pieces of flat dough in your pan let fry for about 4 to 5 minutes on each side or until golden brown then remove from pan.

Frozies

1) Pre-heat your deep fryer to about 350° (make sure it's an approved deep fryer, not on the stove top)

2) Cut small pieces of dough and shape into balls, after you've prepared about six pieces, place in hot oil and let fry for about 5 minutes or until golden brown.

3) Remove from oil and let drain on some paper towel or parchment paper for a minute, then place in a bowl and sprinkle them with some icing sugar and cinnamon. You also can cut them a little and add some jam or jelly to the centre.

Note from Bonita:
Try the toutons with jam or molasses (a Newfoundland favourite)! Also, fry an egg over easy, cut open one of your toutons and place the egg in the middle for a unique egg sandwich. My son & his wife enjoy toutons with coconut milk! You can also enjoy toutons with baked beans or just a bit of butter :)

BOLOGNA STEW

Serves 4

Bonita's Tip: *Serve this dish with bread or rolls; it helps soak up all the sauce!*

INGREDIENTS

2 Cups Bologna

1 Medium Onion

2 Medium Potatoes

2 Carrots

1 Medium Turnip

2 Sticks Celery

4 Tbsp Ketchup

½ Tsp Pepper

2 Tbsp Worcestershire Sauce

1 Tbsp Butter

½ Tsp Olive oil

1) Chop bologna and vegetables in large cubes. Dice onions in small pieces.

2) Preheat a large frying pan on medium heat, add butter and olive oil, add diced onion. Let fry until onion starts to cook, add bologna, continue frying until golden brown.

3) Reduce heat to low then add ketchup, Worcestershire sauce and pepper, continue cooking for another few minutes, remove from heat.

4) In another large preheated pot, add vegetables and olive oil, fry until vegetables are golden brown. Add bologna and onion mixture.

5) Mix together, top with warm or hot water (to cover vegetables).

6) Continue cooking on medium heat for ½ hour or until vegetables are tender or almost cooked.

Taste sauce; if want more flavour, add more ketchup, Worcestershire sauce, pepper or salt.

Bonita's Tip:
I didn't put any salt in this recipe because I felt it wasn't necessary. You may also customize your flavours by adding more of your favourite veggies or spices.

This recipe for Bologna Stew can also be done in a slow cooker on low heat. Start by frying your meat and onions, adding the sauces and spices, then combine it all in your slow cooker for a few hours until you are ready to serve it.

CABBAGE ROLLS

Pre-heat oven 350° / **Prep time** 1 hour / **Cook time** 1 ½ Hours / **Serves** 6

Bonita's Tip: Green cabbage works well with this dish. Ask your local farmers' stand for some.

INGREDIENTS

1 ½ lbs lean ground beef

1 ½ cups rice

1 medium onion

2 cloves garlic

½ tsp pepper

Pinch salt

½ cup salt beef, small pieces

1 cup water

1 can tomato sauce

1 can tomatoes

2 small carrots

1 medium green cabbage

1) Half fill a large boiler with cold water, place full cabbage in boiler, add a pinch of salt, bring water to a boil.

2) Parboil cabbage until leafs are soft, cut each cabbage leaf off with a fork and knife and put on a plate to cool. To avoid burning yourself, you may remove the cabbage from the boiler in order to cut leaves.

3) Cut salt beef into small cubes, remove excess fat from beef, place in another small boiler, cook for about 1 hour.

4) In large bowl, add ground beef, rice, chopped onion, garlic, grated carrots, onion powder, salt and pepper, ½ can tomato sauce, ½ can tomatos and chopped pre-cooked salt beef. Mix all ingredients together.

5) Begin by taking one cabbage leaf, scoop ¼ cup beef and rice mixture into each leaf, roll it away from yourself, repeat until all cabbage and beef and rice mixture is used.

6) In large roaster, layer each cabbage roll one way then the second layer the opposite direction, top with remainder of tomato sauce and a cup of cold water, pinch salt and pepper.

7) Cover roaster with a lid or foil wrap, place in your pre-heated oven for about 1½ hours, then when cooked remove from the oven. Plate and top with sauce. Serve your cabbage rolls on their own or with perogies and garlic sausage.

RHUBARB & STRAWBERRY JAM

Prep time 10 mins / **Cook time** 1 hour 15 mins / **Canning time** 10 min / **Serves** Family

Bonita's Tip: Make this jam in season and bottle it for the long winter.

1) In large saucepan combine all ingredients, start the boil on a medium heat cook for around 10 to 15 minutes then reduce heat to low.

2) Continue cooking on a low heat for one hour, stirring occasionally so jam doesn't burn, while waiting for jam to cook, start to prepare your mason bottles.

3) Soak three to four one-cup bottles, lids and caps in hot water for 10 minutes.

4) Remove from hot water, place upside down on a towel until ready to use.

INGREDIENTS

4 Cups rhubarb cubed

2 Cups strawberries

2 Cups sugar

1 tsp freshly squeezed lemon & zest

5) When jam have cooked check it by spooning up a tsp full and placing it on a cool plate, if the jam stays thick and don't run off start scooping it in your mason jars.

6) After clean around your bottle rims and start to cap, placing caps and lids on bottles making sure to tighten each one.

7) Leave at room temperature over night or 12 hours. Check each bottle to see if they are sealed, if not, store jam in the fridge. If sealed, store in a cool room; date and label each bottle.

BLUEBERRY JAM

Prep time 20 mins / **Cook time** 30 mins / **Canning time** 10 min / **Serves** Family

Bonita's Tip: *Pre soak your mason jars and lids in hot water for about 10 min, remove from water let drip dry on a cloth. If you are using frozen berries let them thaw.*

1) In a medium saucepan, add blueberries, lemon juice and zest, let berries start to boil on a low heat, then add sugar stir until all dissolved.

2) Start mashing your blueberries to help brake them down.

3) Continue cooking on a medium heat until your berries start to condense and thicken.

4) Depending on how thick you like your jam, you can add certo or pectin, optional.

When your jam has cooked for about 30 minutes, remove from heat and start scooping hot jam into mason jars. Clean tops of mason jars to remove any blueberries, place lids and caps on each one, tighten.

INGREDIENTS

4 Cups of fresh or frozen blueberries (thaw)

2 Tsp lemon and lemon zest

3 Cups White sugar

2 Tsp Certo or fruit jell pectin (optional)

This mixture makes 3 cups of jam or 4 small mason jars. If you would only like to have the jelly part of your jam, just strain your mixture through a strainer, pressing down on your berries to get all the juice. Pour in each mason jar and continue the steps above.

Bonita's Tip:
Date and label each bottle. Cool for 6 hours or over night at room temperature. Store in a cool place or in your fridge, when you are ready to open your mason jars, refrigerate until used.

FISH CAKES

Yields 12 medium fish cakes / **Serves** 4 to 6

Bonita's Tip: Fry up a few fish cakes and save the rest, uncooked, in a freezer bag. Date them for enjoying at another time!

INGREDIENTS

1 ½ cups boneless salt cod
4 Tbsp Butter
3 tsp olive oil
1 medium onion
6 medium potatoes
1 large egg
2 Tbsp Savoury
Pinch pepper
Sea salt optional

1) Soak your salt cod overnight, drain water.

2) In medium boiler half full with water, add fish.

3) In another medium boiler half full with water. Add ½ tsp sea salt (optional). Add ½ medium onion, then add potatoes.

4) In a frying pan, add 1 tsp butter, 1 tsp olive oil, melt then add remaining onion, fry until golden brown.

5) When fish and potatoes are cooked, drain water.

6) In a large bowl, add potatoes, sautéd onion, savoury, egg, pepper; mash together.

7) Before adding your fish, flake it apart with a fork, make sure there are no bones in your fish.

8) After you have all your fish flaked, add to your bowl continue mashing to mix all your ingredients together.

9) In a small bowl add ½ cup of flour, then start scooping your mixture up with a ice cream scoop, to make equal helpings.

10) Form each scoop of fish mixture into a flat patty then roll in your flour and put to the side on a plate until all your fish cakes are made.

11) Preheat a medium frying pan, add 1 tsp butter and 1 tsp olive oil. Place about four fish cakes in pan, let fry until golden brown on each side.

PAN FRIED COD FILETS

Serves 4 to 6

Bonita's Tip: You can omit the bread crumbs if you'd prefer to fry the fish in flour only.

INGREDIENTS

6 pieces cod filets

1 large egg

1 cup 2% milk

1 cup stale bread crumbs

1 cup flour

1 tbsp salt

1 tbsp pepper

1 tsp onion powder

1 tbsp olive oil

1 tsp garlic powder or freshly chopped

Try our fan favourite "Cod Au Gratin" at
bonitaskitchen.com/cod

1) In a bowl mix egg and milk together, add a pinch of your seasonings.

2) In another dish, add bread crumbs.

3) In another dish, add flour and a pinch of your seasonings together.

4) Season your cod with a pinch of salt, pepper, onion powder and garlic.

5) Start rolling your cod in the egg mixture, roll your cod in the bread crumbs, roll in your flour mixture.

6) Preheat your frying pan on medium heat for a couple minutes, add 1 tbsp of olive oil & butter, after it starts to warm, place your cod filets in pan, start frying.

7) Fry cod for 5 minutes on one side or until golden brown.

8) Flip to other side and fry for another 5 minutes or until golden brown.

After you've fried all the filets, season again if needed, if you are not ready to serve your cod, put in glass plate and place in your oven at 170°, uncovered.

9) This will prevent your cod from going soggy and it will stay crisp.

HOMEMADE BREAD

Prep time 10 mins / **Mix time** 10 mins / **Rise time** 2x 30 mins / **Bake time** 30 - 40 mins / **Serves** Family

Bonita's Tip: Preheat oven at 350º, bake bread for 30 minutes or until golden brown, when baked take out of your pans and place it out on a rack (resting rack). This prevents bread from getting moist on the bottom. Glaze bread with butter then cover with a towel.
Watch the video online: **bonitaskitchen.com/bread**

INGREDIENTS

8 ½ cups White or Wheat flour

2 Tbsp yeast

¼ cup melted butter

½ tsp salt

2 tbsp sugar

2 ½ cups warm water

1) Combine in large bowl, 8 cups flour, 1 tbsp sugar and 1tsp salt, mix together.

2) In another bowl, add dry fast rising yeast with ½ cup warm water and 1 tbsp sugar, let rise for a few minutes.

3) In another bowl add 2 cups of warm water and melt 2 tbsp of butter and combine together.

4) Pour yeast over flour mixture in bowl, add warm water and butter, mixing all ingredients together with a spoon or your hand until thick. Continue adding flour to work dough together with your hands.

5) Knead dough, add more flour if necessary until dough is smooth, elastic and no longer sticky. You may hear "cracking" of the dough when folding. Keep working dough into a ball.

6) When complete, sprinkle some flour over the top. I always draw the sign of the cross a few times on top, then cut a cross into the top of the dough (optional). Cover with wax paper or parchment paper and a towel.

7) Let rise in a warm place until dough rises for half an hour, then knead down. Repeat step, allow dough to rise again for another ½ hour.

8) After your dough rises, cut in pieces forming it inwards into a ball. Place in your bread pans; make three buns per pan. You can also have one piece to make a loaf of garlic bread or bread buns, and toutons/bankers.

9) Makes 3 loaves of bread, keep covered in a warm place until bread rises half the size you started with. Once loaves have risen to desired size, bake in oven at 350º for 30 minutes, or until golden brown. When complete, place on a cooling rack, glaze with butter, cover with a dishtowel.

Serves Family

1) In a medium bowl, add 2 cups of white pea beans, top with cold water, add ½ tsp sea salt, cover, soak over night.

2) When ready, you will need a cast iron pot or ceramic pot with cover.

3) Chop onions and add to the bottom of your pot, drain all excess water off beans, top with new cold water and boil for 1 ½ hours on medium heat with cover partially open.

4) When boiling is complete, drain water into a container and keep for soup or baking. Add the beans to cast iron pot.

5) Add 5 cups of cold water to your pot. In a small bowl mix together the remainder of your ingredients, except fat pork or bacon.

6) Pour over onions and beans in pot, mix together then top with fat pork or bacon.

7) Put lid on bake pot then place in a 325° oven for 3 ½ to 4 hours. Check half way through the bake time, add more water if needed, cover and continue baking.

INGREDIENTS

2 Medium onions

5 Cups cold water

2 Tsp Vinegar of choice

1 Tbsp Brown sugar

1 Tsp Mustard

¼ Cup Molasses

½ Cup Ketchup

Pinch black pepper

½ Tsp sea salt

1 Cup chopped fat pork or bacon

2 Cups White pea beans

Bonita's Tip: This recipe serves eight people. If you'd like more, double the recipe. Baked beans can take a long time to make, I reduced bake time by adding an extra hour on the boiling process.

When baked beans are done, remove from heat, serve hot or cold. If you'd like to bottle them, just follow the canning process. Always label and date your bottles before storing them.

SPLIT PEA SOUP (WITH DOUGHBOYS)

Serves 6

INGREDIENTS

Soup

2 cups split peas

1 onion, chopped

1 cup celery, diced

1 cup potato, diced

½ turnip, diced

3 carrots, diced

1 lb salt beef
or 1 lb spare ribs
or hambone (with meat on the
bone)

1) Soak salt beef or spare ribs overnight in cold water. In a separate container, soak peas overnight in cold water.

2) Drain water from both containers. In medium boiler, add fresh water, onion, salt beef or spare ribs, peas. Simmer for 2 hours.

3) After cooking for 1 ½ hours, add vegetables to boiler.

Bonita's Tip:
Peas cooked in a cotton bag with your boiled jiggs dinner can also be used for your soup. Add left over peas in a medium pot with vegetables and some broth. Simmer for 20 mins.

Doughboys

1 ½ cups flour

¼ cup butter (softened)

3 teaspoons baking powder

1 teaspoon salt

½ - ¾ cup water or
½ - ¾ cup milk

1) In a small bowl, combine butter, flour, baking powder and salt.

2) Mix in water or milk, to soften dough.

3) Drop a teaspoon-sized dough ball into soup, repeat until all dough is used. Cover pot tightly, cook for 15 minutes.

TEABUNS

Serves 8 / **Yields** 24 buns / **Prep time** 15 mins / **Bake time** 15 mins / **Preheat oven** 350º

1) Mix all dry ingredients into a bowl, then add pieces of cold butter and mix well together.

2) Mix egg and milk together in another bowl and add to mixture working it in with your hand until almost into a ball.

3) Add raisins if you are making the raisin buns, if not, don't add.

4) Continue on forming into a ball then put out onto a piece of wax paper or parchment paper.

5) Cover with a sprinkle of flour and roll into ¼ inch thick pastry.

With a 2 inch cookie cutter, cut out 24 buns, place on a greased cookie pan or square pan, place in the oven for 15 minutes or until golden brown.

INGREDIENTS

Plain Buns

2 Cups white or wheat flour

½ Cup white sugar

¼ tsp salt

½ cup cold butter

½ cup carnation milk

4 tsp baking powder

1 egg

Raisins Buns

½ cup raisins

Bonita's Tip:
Once baking is complete, remove from oven put on a serving plate eat hot or cold with butter and homemade jam.

Watch the video online:
bonitaskitchen.com/teabuns

21

CHERRY CAKE

Prep time 15 mins / **Bake time** 45 mins / **Yields** 1 round cake or 2 loaf cakes / **Serves** 8-10

Bonita's Tip: *Don't over bake your cherry cake as it will become too dry. Double the recipe* for more cake!

INGREDIENTS

1 ½ Cups Butter
1 ½ Cups Sugar
3 Eggs
1 Tsp Vanilla
3 Cups Flour
1 ½ Tsp Baking Powder
1 Cup Carnation Milk (room temp.)
1 Cup Halved Glacé Cherries
(roll in 1/3 cup flour before adding to mixture)

1) Cream together butter and sugar.

2) Add eggs, one at a time. mix well until light and fluffy.

3) Mix in vanilla.

4) In another bowl sift or mix together flour and baking powder.

5) Folding dry ingredients with creamed mixture, don't over mix, then slowly add room temp milk to your mixture.

6) Fold cherries that have been rolled in flour to your mixture. Grease one springform pan or two loaf pans.

7) Bake in a 350° preheated oven for 45 minutes to 1 hour, depending on your oven. Always check the middle of your cake first with a toothpick before removing it from the oven, if it comes out dry it's done; if wet, close door and leave for another five minutes, check again.

8) Remove cake from oven, let set in cake pan for 5 to 10 minutes before removing. You may need to run a knife around the sides to remove from pan if stuck.

BLUEBERRY & CREAM TRIFLE

Serves 8 - 10

Bonita's Tip: This dish for blueberries and cream trifle will make a perfert dessert for any occasion. You can use fresh or frozen blueberries. "My Favourite"!

INGREDIENTS

Berry Mixture:

2 Cups Fresh or Frozen blueberries
2 Tbsp Sugar
2 Tbsp Cornstarch
¼ Cup Cold water
½ Tbsp lemon juice

Filling:

1 Angel food cake chopped in cubes

1 Pk Cream cheese

2/3 Cup half & half or evaporated milk

2/3 Cup Sugar

Whipping Cream:

1 ½ Cups Heavy whipping Cream

3 Tbsp Icing Sugar

1) In a medium saucepan, cook berry mixture until thickened, 5-7 minutes, let cool to room temperature.

2) In a large bowl, whip together cream cheese, milk and sugar until smooth and creamy.

3) Fold in angel food cake cubes until they are all thickly coated with this mixture.

4) In another bowl, whip together heavy whipping cream and icing sugar.

5) In a large glass bowl, layer your ingredients. Spread half of your angel food mixture in the bottom of your bowl, top with half of your blueberry sauce, then top with half whipping cream.

6) Repeat Step 5 once more. Top with fresh blueberries, cover with plastic wrap then refrigerate for at lease 2 hours before serving.

INDEX

I want to thank you from the bottom of my heart for sharing my journey on Bonita's Kitchen! I hope you and your family will enjoy the recipes in my cookbook for years to come.

From my kitchen to yours,
Bonita

FOR MORE NEWFOUNDLAND RECIPES & INSTRUCTIONAL VIDEOS, VISIT...
BONITASKITCHEN.COM

Printed in the USA
CPSIA information can be obtained
at www.ICGtesting.com
LVRC091041251123
764678LV00059B/115

9 780995 346802